Riders, Teams and Stadiums of the 70s

by Keith Lawson

Better
  Than
    Nothing

Riders, Teams and Stadiums of the 70s

Published by Better Than Nothing, Poole, Dorset, UK. 2018

Printed by lulu.com

Copyright © Keith Lawson 2018   All Rights Reserved

ISBN 978-0-244-72538-9

Other books by Keith Lawson (see back of this book for more information)
"Rebels 1975 – The Last Season"   (2018) ISBN 978-0-244-99725-0
"The Cheetahs 1976 – Resurrection" (2018) ISBN 978-0-244-699934-5

While the publisher and the author have used their best efforts in preparing this book, they make no representations or warranties with respect to the accuracy or the completeness of the contents of this book.
Any request to reproduce any part of this book or for photographs to be supplied should be addressed to sppaonline@gmail.com

The photos reproduced in this book are not of the standard that is possible today with digital cameras. Back then we used "fast" film, typically 400ASA which produces a grainy effect, especially the more the photo is enlarged. And we couldn't always get the exposure perfect – light conditions changing by the minute in stadiums with low quality lamps (compared to modern standards). Added to which (mea culpa), I didn't store the negatives well, thinking they were only useful for the immediate time, not foreseeing a nostalgia and a new media of internet. So there are scratches and other defects and not all can be erased by editing software. Publications would only take the best photos, so there must be many that didn't make to press, but they exist and tell a story that is better to be told than not. Here are some of mine

CONTENTS
The Riders

Foreword

Martin Ashby

Carl Askew

Terry Betts

Nigel Boocock

John Boulger

Barry Briggs

Peter Collins

Phil Crump

John Davis

John Dews

Trevor Geer

Richard Greer

Bert Harkins

Rickard Hellsen

Tommy Jansson

Pete Jarman

Dave Jessup

Gordon Kennett

Bob Kilby

Michael Lee

John Louis

Dag Lovaas

Ulf Lovaas

Jim McMillan

Ivan Mauger

Anders Michanek

Chris Morton

Dave Morton

Ole Olsen

Joe Owen

Malcolm Simmons

Ray Wilson

Martin Yeates

CONTENTS

The Teams and Stadiums

Belle Vue Aces

Coventry Bees

Cradley Heath

Eastbourne Eagles

Exeter Falcons

Hackney Hawks

Halifax Dukes

Hull Vikings

Ipswich Witches

Kings Lynn Stars

Leicester Lions

Newcastle Diamonds

Newport United (Wasps)

Oxford Cheetahs

Oxford Rebels

Peterborough Panthers

Poole Pirates

Reading Racers

Sheffield Tigers

Swindon Robins

Weymouth Wizards

White City Rebels

Wimbledon Dons

Wolverhampton Wolves

FOREWORD

I attended my first speedway meeting as a boy when a grown-up cousin, visiting us for a holiday, took me to see the Oxford Cheetahs. All I can remember is the noise, the vibration and the smell and I was hooked. Unfortunately, I didn't have the money to attend as often as I would have liked and there would be a clash with school (early to bed) and homework. The names that gave me the thrills were Arne Pander, Ove Fundin (strange exotic names of non-Brits) and riders such as Ronnie Genz and Colin Gooddy. Speedway was a melting pot of people from overseas and home-grown talent.

Once school was out of the way and I was in a job, I became a regular at Sandy Lane and would occasionally get to Away meetings and sample the joys of other stadiums. There was a gang of us, on the stands, (near the bar), more or less in line with the start. There was banter with visiting fans – they could give as good as they got and nothing malicious or a threat of violence. Cradley fans could be the most vocal – they always seemed to have a good following. Local Derbies with Swindon were always fun.

Then, in 1973, in the next street to where I lived, a free newspaper (a novel idea at the time) was started in an old teddy bear factory – The Oxford Journal. I went in and offered to write a speedway column and the editor said to submit and he would see. A big problem was deadline was Tuesday and the match night was Thursday, paper out on Friday. One answer was to go to more away meetings, which were not so well reported in the Oxford Mail; my first ever interview was in Hackney pits with Malcolm Ballard. The Journal then set up a regular column with Bob Kilby, so my input was not required and I extended my journalistic efforts to other sports.

Covering other sports earned me a halfpenny a word – and I could submit, say, 500 words, and the editor would chop it down. So not a big earner. But I had realised that he liked stories with photos and I used to invite their staff photographer along as my story was more likely to be printed. It wasn't long before I twigged that the photographer had the better deal. He would get paid per photo whether it was big or passport sized. And he didn't have to remember a lot of detail.

I was working at the central Post Office in St Aldates, Oxford, and a few doors down was a independent photographic shop. The proprietor was very helpful and I came away with a Zenith SLR, two lenses (one wide angle and one telephoto), an enlarger and the paraphernalia to set up a darkroom (which was the bathroom at home). A book on photography to teach me about how to use the camera (focal length, exposures, etc.) and how to develop film and photos was how I learned, with trial and error.

So I had become a photographer!

At one meeting, the editor of another new free paper – The Oxford Review – asked me to contribute, so I had two locals and I would also send away to the Speedway Star. The Oxford Review would go through several transformations, ultimately going bust and leaving me unpaid for all the work I had done.

In 1974, I had assumed the role of Trackside Photographer for the Rebels and had a good relationship with promoters Danny Dunton and Bob Dugard. I supplied them with photos for the programmes and even designed a few covers. I sent a collection of photos to the Mirror Group for their library and, once in a while, a cheque would come through the post when they used one of my photos. A better customer was D.C. Thomson, publisher of Commando comics; they used photos of sports men and women inside their covers and paid very well.

1975 was a bigger year and the year when the Rebels became a force, winning the Midland Cup and looking like a team that would rise to the top. I have covered this in my book "The Rebels 1975 – The Last Season", which was when the stadium was expected to close and the team would move to White City for 1976.

A winter of lobbying by the SOS Committee (of which I was a member) and the fans secured a future for speedway in Oxford but without their beloved riders. My second book "The Cheetahs 1976 – The Resurrection" tells the story of the fight and the season for a New National League team, promoted by Harry Bastable and Tony Allsopp.

So, here is my third book. It's about my heroes – all the men who donned leather and rode those speed machines with no brakes - in my period as a photographer. My photos today are in great demand with the rise of digital media and the internet. I supply Wikipedia and helped create entries for riders who hadn't already been listed (which is ongoing work). A Google search of keith lawson speedway will throw up countless sites who use my photos. Today, I have my own website - https://l4w50n.wixsite.com/sppaonline – as I still do photography, but across a broad range of interests.

I am no Mike Patrick or Alf Weedon, going to tracks around the country and overseas, and I freely admit I am not in their class; I mostly followed my team and a couple of others. Here are photos from those times – to provoke memories for riders and fans.
I hope you enjoy this tribute to those legends of the 70s.

Keith Lawson 2018

PS as a bonus – some photos from 2016 and 2018 as I renewed my contact with the speedway family

MARTIN ASHBY

(born 5 February 1944, Marlborough, Wiltshire).

In a career spanning the years 1961 to 1980, Martin rode for three teams – Swindon Robins, Exeter Falcons and Reading Racers – but it is as a Robin he is best remembered and that was the team I associate with him as it coincides with my period of journalism.

He reached the final of the Speedway World Championship in 1968; came third with Nigel Boocock in the World Pairs in 1969; and was in the Great Britain team that won in 1968 and again in 1975.

1976

1974

Partnering Ulf Lovaas at Radio Oxford Best Pairs 1975

MARTIN ASHBY

Fun at Blunsdon on sponsor's moped 1974

WC Semi_Final at Leicester 21 May 1974 with Peter Collins and Barry Briggs

WC Semi_Final at Leicester 21 May 1974 with Billy Sanders and Reg Wilson

MARTIN ASHBY

Martin with Mike Broadbank

Martin with Malcolm Simmons

1975 guest rider for Ole Olsen at Oxford

Swindon Silver Plume 1975 with Dag Lovaas and Norman Hunter

CARL ASKEW

(born 19 November 1952, Sydney, Australia).

A flamboyant presence, Carl brought some excitement to the newly reformed Oxford Cheetahs in 1976, missing 1977 (to ride for Stoke Potters) but returning for the following two years before retiring in 1979.

His first British club was Birmingham Brummies and he also had rides with Wolverhampton Wolves, Cradley United and Sheffield Tigers.

Returning to Australia, Carl continued his love of bikes in various sports (Long Track and Drag Racing) as well as restoration.

Second time as a Cheetah – 1978

1976

1978

See more of Carl in "The Cheetahs 1976 – The Resurrection" (2018)

TERRY BETTS

(born 15 September 1943, Harlow, Essex)

Career spanned from 1960 to 1979, riding for Norwich Stars, Wolverhampton Wolves, Long Eaton Archers, King's Lynn Stars and Reading Racers. It is as a King's Lynn Star he is most remembered, riding there from 1965 to 1978 and voted as the greatest Stars' rider of all time by the club's fans.

Terry became World Pairs Champion with Ray Wilson on 1972, was in the winning Great Britain team in 1972 and 1973, winning the World Team Cup. He reached the final of the World Championship in 1974.

Guest rider for Dag Lovaas at Oxford

TERRY BETTS

England v Young Lions 6 September 1976

Birthday cake presentation from the team away at Reading 1976

NIGEL BOOCOCK

(born 17 September 1937, Wakefield, Yorkshire. Died 3 April 2015, Queensland, Australia)

Career spanned from 1955 to 1979. His longest stint was as a Coventry Bee (1959 – 1976) where he is remembered as one of the greats.

Booey appeared in eight World Championships and was in the team that won the World Team Cup in 1968.

Other teams he rode for: Bradford Tudors (1955-1957), Birmingham Brummies (1957), Ipswich Witches (1958), Bristol Bulldogs (1977-1978), Exeter Falcons (1979-1980), and Canterbury Crusaders (1979).

JOHN BOULGER

(born 18 June 1945, Adelaide, Australia)

John rode for only three teams – started his career with Long Eaton Archers (1967) who would move to Leicester where John would have two stints as a Lion (1968-1973, 1977-1979) separated by a period with Cradley United (1974-1976).

Came second, with Phil Crump, in the 1974 World Pairs behind Anders Michanek and Soren Sjosten.

Rode as captain with the winning Australian side in the World Team Cup 1976.

BARRY BRIGGS, MBE

(born 30 December 1934, Christchurch, New Zealand)

Four times World Champion – 1957, 1958, 1964, and 1966. Truly one of the Greats, Briggo appeared in 17 consecutive World Individual Championship finals – a record – and an eighteenth later.

Associated mostly with two teams – Swindon Robins (1964-1972) and Wimbledon Dons (1952-1959 and 1974-1975) – he also rode for New Cross Rangers (1960), Southampton Saints (1961-1963), and Hull Vikings (1976).

Keith Lawson

PETER COLLINS MBE

(born 24 March 1954, Manchester)

One of the greatest British speedway riders – World Champion (1976), World Pairs (1977, 1980, 1983, 1984), and World Team Cup (1973, 1974, 1975, 1977, 1980).

Started his career as a Rochdale Hornet in 1971 but then was with Belle Vue Aces from 1971-1986.

1975

PETER COLLINS MBE

1976

With Eric Boocock 1976

PHIL CRUMP

(born 9 February 1952, Mildura, Victoria, Australia)

Many would agree, Crump is the World Champion who never was, such was his talent. He came third in 1976 in the individual World Championship and won, as a member of the Australian team, the World Team Cup in the same year.

His British career started with Crewe Kings (1971-1972) but is best remembered as a Newport Wasp (1971, 1974-1976). His father-in-law was Neil Street, who developed a four valve engine that revolutionised racing.

Phil also had outings with Wolverhampton Wolves, Oxford Cheetahs and Hackney Hawks in 1971 – showing how much in demand he was. Regular team places with King's Lynn Stars (1971-1973), Bristol Bulldogs (1977-1978) and Swindon Robins (1979-1986 and 1990).

JOHN DAVIS

(born 10 November 1954, Oxford).

John certainly thought about image when racing, bringing some glamour with his attention to appearance and stylish leathers. His career started with Peterborough Panthers (1971-1973) followed by riding for a number of teams in the British League: Poole Pirates (1971, 1981-1983), Oxford Cheetahs/Rebels (1971-1974), Reading Racers (1975-1981, 1985-1987), Sheffield Tigers (1983), Wimbledon Dons (1984), King's Lynn Stars (1988-1989), and Swindon Robins (1989-1991). He was a member of the winning World Team Cup Team in 1977, and was capped for England 68 times. On the continent, he was the first Englishman to race in the Polish League (Gdansk) and the first to win the Czech Golden Helmet. He spent 10 seasons in the German League, winning four titles.

1974 riding for Oxford at home to Poole Pirates (with Colin Gooddy)

JOHN DEWS

(born 26 March 1945, Wakefield, Yorkshire. Died 7 August 1995).

Never in the top rank, but John proved his worth as team rider for Belle Vue Aces (1962-1963), Sheffield Tigers (1962-1970), Wimbledon Dons (1971-1972), Oxford Rebels (1973-1975) [where I got to know a really nice guy], and with White City Rebels (1976).

It was with the Oxford Rebels that John had two highlights in his career – winning the Radio Oxford Best Pairs with Richard Greer (1974) and the Midland Cup (1975). After retiring from active racing, he became team manager at Sheffield (1977-1980). Over his career he rode 277 matches, with a match average of 6.29.

Winner (with Richard Greer) of the Radio Oxford Best Pairs 1974
Bob Radford on mike and sponsor on left

TREVOR GEER

(born 24 June 1953, Polegate, East Sussex).

Trevor started his career with Eastbourne Eagles in the early 70s and would have rides for Oxford Rebels (both promoted by Bob Dugard) and started his full-time British League career in 1975, being part of the Midland Cup winning team.

He transferred with the Rebels to White City in 1976 and was part of the British League topping team in 1977.

Trevor makes it into this book because he was such a nice guy and a real trier on the track.

RICHARD GREER

(born 29 November 1946, Peterborough, Cambridgeshire)

Probably the most popular Peterborough Panther rider of all time. But I knew Richard at Oxford, where he was a great team rider and a guy who enjoyed his speedway. A highlight was his Radio Oxford Best Pairs (1974) win with John Dews, with some immaculate team riding. Ole Olsen and Trevor Geer came second. Then, in 1975, he was in the Midland Cup winning team when Oxford beat Wolves away in the final. He transferred to White City in 1976 when the Rebels moved form Oxford. Birmingham Brummies had his services 1977 – 1978 before he returned to Peterborough 1979-1981. After finishing as a rider, Richard still was involved at the County Ground and is still active with the World Speedway Riders Association (WSRA).

RICHARD GREER

With John Davis, 1974

Oxford

BERT HARKINS

(born 15 April 1940, Govan, Glasgow)

One of the great characters of speedway, the "Haggis" (aka "Bertola") rode in Britain, South Africa, Australia and the USA.

Remembered best for two teams: Edinburgh Monarchs (1962-1966, 1977, 1978-79) and Wimbledon Dons (1973-1975, 1979) where he could be devastating when paired in heats with Barry Briggs.

Today, he is active with the National Speedway Museum and the World Speedway Riders Association (WSRA).

2017

At Oxford 1974

1974 with Barry Briggs

RICKARD HELLSEN

(born 1 June 1951, Stockholm, Sweden).

A successful rider in Sweden. His career spanned the years 1972-1992.

In the British League, he was one of the Midland Cup winning Oxford Rebels (1975) and League Champions White City Rebels (1977).

1975

Keith Lawson

1976

1975

More on Rickard's 1975 season in "Rebels 1975 – The Last Season" lulu.com/shop

GEORGE HUNTER

(born 30 January 1939, Ladybank, Fife. Died 11 May 1999)

Apart from being Scottish Open Champion in 1964 and part of Wolverhampton Wolves Midland Cup winning team in 1973, no honours came George's way but he is fondly remembered as a team rider and character. His first club was Motherwell (1958) but his time with the Edinburgh Monarchs was a major part of this career, riding in 360 league matches. Other teams on his CV include Coatbridge Monarchs, Newcastle Diamonds, Glasgow Tigers, Wolverhampton Wolves, Oxford Cheetahs and Berwick Bandits.

1974

1975 challenging Gordon Kennett in a Midland Cup final

TOMMY JANSSON

(born 2 October 1952. Died 20 May 1976).

One of the most promising riders of his generation and tragically died in a racing accident in a World Championship Qualifying Round.

Made his first appearance in the UK in 1970, on tour with a Swedish team. Came back to race with Wembley Lions in 1971 but that only lasted for three matches.

Then, in 1972 he appeared for Wimbledon Dons, the British team he is most associated with (1972-1973, 1975-1976) the break in 1974 due to a ban on Swedish riders. Winner of World Pairs in 1973 and 1975 with Anders Michanek.

Bo Jansson, Rickard Hellsen and Tommy

PETE JARMAN

(born 30 June 1935, Brockley, London. Died 23 July 2007).

I think of Pete as "old school" - those tough characters that epitomised the sport. His partnerships with Colin Gooddy were so memorable as "no surrender, no prisoners".

Speedy was a cycle speedway kid who moved into the professional sport with rides for Eastbourne Eagles, Stoke Potters, Wolverhampton Wolves, Oxford Cheetahs/Rebels and Cradley Heathens.

After hanging up his leathers, he stayed involved in the sport, doing track maintenance, coaching and running a speedway school at Cowley.

1976

DAVE JESSUP

(born 7 March 1953, Ipswich, Suffolk)

Another of the few who would be voted as the world champion who wasn't; a long list of individual honours but not the top one, his best position was runner-up in 1980 to Michael Lee. As a team member, he did win World Team Cups in 1974, 1977, and 1980. Plus Best Pairs, partnering Peter Collins in 1980.

A graduate of Eastbourne Eagles (1969) he would ride for West Ham Hammers, Wembley Lions, Leicester Lions, Reading Racers, King's Lynn Stars, Wimbledon Dons and finally Mildenhall Fen Tigers.

1975

GORDON KENNETT

(born 2 September 1953)

A graduate of Eastbourne and a nearly World Champion.

A long career over 24 years riding for Eastbourne Eagles, Wimbledon Dons, Leicester Lions, Hackney Hawks, Cradley Heathens then established team places with Oxford then White City Rebels, winning the Midland Cup in 1975 and topping the League in 1977.

He was runner-up to Ole Olsen in the 1978 World Championship and won Best Pairs with Malcolm Simmons that same year.

1976

BOB KILBY

(born 23 September 1944, Swindon, Wilts. Died 11 January 2009)

Think of Bob Kilby and you think of Swindon Robins (1964-1970, 1975-1980, 1983) but he also had short spells at Exeter Falcons (1971-1973) and Oxford Rebels (1973-1974). An incredible 2,226 rides in 556 meetings but a shortage of personal trophies, instead working as a team rider to secure the Midland Cup twice (1967, 1968) for the Robins and a British League table top in 1967. Bob would have nicknames for people, mine was "Snappy". His brother, Mick, was a photographer and a companion of the centre green whose company I enjoyed. His son, Lee, wrote a biography of his father "To the Heart of Kilb" and is heavily involved with Swindon Speedway.

Keith Lawson

MICHAEL LEE

(born 11 December 1958, Cambridge)

An incredible talent, winning a host of individual awards, including the World Team Cup (1977, 1980), the World Championship in 1980 and the World Long Track in 1981.

Only starting his career in 1975 with Boston Barracudas, two years later he was the top scorer in the British League with an average of 10.64. He enjoyed a long career spell with King's Lynn Stars and two years at Poole Pirates (1983-1984). Such a short time in speedway which was the result of a ban for a racing incident (1984) which many think was a conspiracy to get him out of racing.

JOHN LOUIS

(born 14 June 1941, Ipswich)

His first venture with motorbikes was a Scrambler but was tempted to try Speedway when a track opened in his home town in 1969.

It is with Ipswich Witches that Tiger is most associated, riding for them 1970-1980, with two British League titles (1975 and 1976).

He rode for his country and secured three World Team Cups (1972, 1974, and 1975).

He was World Best Pairs Champion in 1976 with Malcolm Simmons.

DAG LOVAAS

(born 25 February 1951, Holmestrand, Norway)

Dag had a short British League career, commencing with Newcastle Diamonds in 1970 and finishing with White City Rebels in 1976.

He was Norwegian Champion in 1973 and 1974 but declined to defend his title in 1975 in favour of success for Oxford Rebels, in the season they won the Midland Cup.

An asset for every team he rode for, with Hackney Hawks (1974) he recorded the highest average in their history.

1975

1975 in Kings Lynn Pits

More on Dag Lovaas in "Rebels 1975 – The Last Season".

ULF LOVAAS

(born 24 March, 1947, Holmestrand, Norway).

The elder brother of Dag and a much loved Oxford Rebel in his second and final year racing in England.

His first BL team was Cradley United (1973).

Doing it before his brother did, Ulf was Norwegian Champion in 1972.

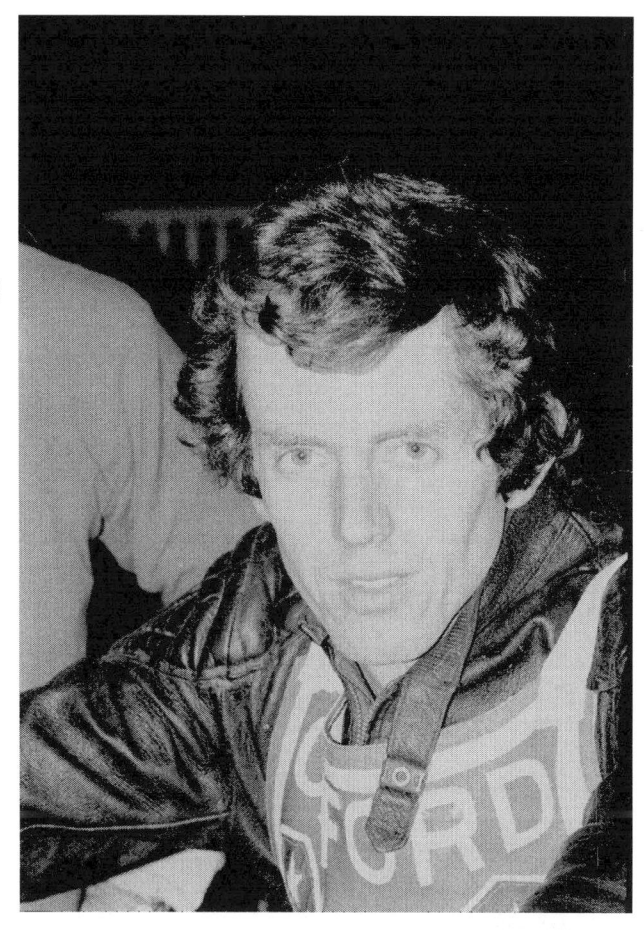

JIM McMILLAN

(born 3 December 1945, Glasgow)

A 20 year career earned him lots of fans. First rode for Glasgow Tigers (1966-1972) (and Coatbridge Tigers 1973) and returned towards the end (1983).

In between he had rides for Hull Vikings (1974-1975), Wolverhampton Wolves (1976-1980), Belle Vue Aces (1981-1982), Oxford Cheetahs (1984) and Berwick Bandits (1984-1986).

Until recently, Jim worked as a machine examiner for the Speedway Control Board.

With Peter Collins at Brandon

IVAN MAUGER OBE

(born 4 October 1939. Died 16 April 2018)

Deemed to have been the greatest ever, the list of titles is impressive – 6 World Championships, 3 Long Track Championships, 2 World Best Pairs, 4 World Team Cups, 4 times British League Champion. His BL career spanned from 1957 (Wimbledon Dons) to 1981 (Hull Vikings) but he continued to race overseas, winning titles in New Zealand. Upon the announcement of his death, there was a surge in the use of my photos of Ivan and I was touched to be contacted by Ivan's daughter, Debbie Pritchard, as a result. Mike Patrick also was grateful to see a photograph I had taken of him with Ivan (we photographers are nearly always behind the camera so usually we are an invisible presence).

IVAN MAUGER OBE

IVAN MAUGER OBE

With Mike Patrick

ANDERS MICHANEK

(born 30 May 1943, Stockholm, Sweden)

Anders was World Champion in 1974 – a difficult task when rivals included Ivan Mauger and Barry Briggs. His first world success was World Team Champions (1970) which he followed with World Best Pairs in 1973, 1974, and 1975, and Long Track 1977.

His longest stint with a BL team was as a Reading Racer (1971-1973, 1975, and 1981). He had single seasons rides with Leicester Lions (1968) although that might count as two as the previous year he rode for Long Eaton Archers, Newcastle Diamonds (1970), Cradley Heath Heathens (1977), and Ipswich Witches (1979).

Keith Lawson Photography

CHRIS MORTON MBE

(born 22 July 1956, Davyhulme, Greater Manchester)

Debuted for Ellesmere Port Gunners in 1973 but was taken into the Belle Vue side following an injury to Chris Pusey.

The Aces is where he spent most of his career (1973-1990). In 1974 he became the British Under-21 Champion.

Successes include World Team Cup (1980), World Best Pairs with Peter Collins (1984) and Ace of Aces Grasstrack Champion (1988).

DAVE MORTON

(born 24 September 1953, Eccles, Lancashire)

First team were Crewe Kings (1971-1974) but had rides before a contract to be a Hackney Hawk (1973-1977).

He transferred to Wolverhampton Wolves (1978-1980), followed by time at Sheffield Tigers (1981-1985).

He was New Zealand Champion in 1975.
His career autobiography is "Tapes, Breaks and Heartaches."

With Dag Lovaas 1974

With John Berry (1976)

OLE OLSEN

(born 16 November 1946)

The Great Dane – a national hero in his homeland. Danish Champion from 1967 to 1981 (with an omission in 1974).

He was World Champion 3 times (1971, 1975, 1978) in an era where his rivals included Barry Briggs and Ivan Mauger. World Team Cup (1978, 1981, 1983). World Pairs (1979) and Midland Cup Champions an incredible 5 times with Wolverhampton Wolves then Coventry Bees.

Possibly the greatest northern hemisphere rider of his era.

1976

JOE OWEN

(born 13 September 1956, Ormskirk, Lancashire)

An exciting rider to watch, he debuted for Barrow Bombers in 1973 where he stayed for two seasons.

1975 saw him at Newcastle Diamonds and again in 1976.

A spell with Hull Vikings (1975-1981) the back to the Diamonds (1982-1984).

While riding for Ellesmere Port Gunners in 1985 he had a career-ending crash.

MALCOLM SIMMONS

(born 20 March 1946. Died 25 May 2014).

A popular rider, Simmo started with Hackney Hawks (1963), moved to West Ham Hammers (1964-1967), then the two clubs with which he is most associated – King's Lynn Stars (1968-1974, 1993) and Poole Pirates (1975-1980).

Other clubs included Wimbledon Dons (1981-1984), Swindon Robins (1985), Hackney Kestrels (1986-1987) and Arena Essex Hammers (1989).

He was a World Team Cup Winner in 1973, 1974, 1975, and 1977. A World Best Pairs champion in 1976, 1977, and 1978. He was runner-up to Peter Collins in the 1976 World Championship.

Keith Lawson

1976

Guesting for Wolves

RAY WILSON

(born 12 March 1947, Merton, Surrey)

Most associated with Leicester Lions (1968-1976) he did ride for Long Eaton Archers (1963-1967) who transferred to Leicester and renamed themselves Lions, and Birmingham Brummies (1977-1979).

He won World Team Cup titles in 1971, 1972, 1973, and 1974, plus a World Best Pairs in 1972 with Terry Betts.

MARTIN YEATES

(born 24 November 1953, Salisbury)

Having had a hand in getting Martin to sign for the Oxford Cheetahs (1977) as go-between of promoters and the ultimate sponsor – Les Windle of Lesandon Drugstores – I could not miss him out.

He had one season at Cowley, went off to spend time as a Poole Pirate, Swindon Robin and Weymouth Wildcat before returning in 1984.

He retired at the end of the 1987 season.

With sponsor, Les Windle and Steve Windle (track mascot)

BELLE VUE ACES

The excitement of following the Rebels on away trips to Manchester was raised by the fact the stadium was inside an amusement park and zoo. Belle Vue Aces were always a team to fear – top class riders with a determination to win every match.

Peter Collins

Soren Sjosten

Kristian Praestbro

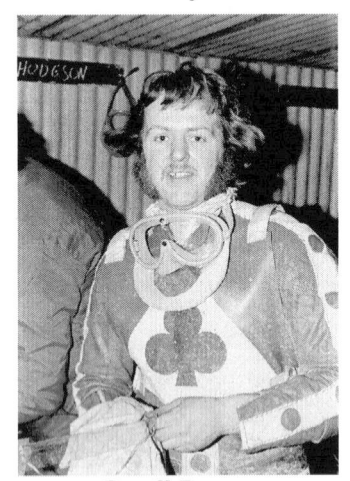

Geoff Pusey

Paul Tyrer

Soren Sjosten leads John Dews (who had also worn the Ace bib in his career)

BELLE VUE ACES   25 April 1974 away at Oxford

Heat 1: Finishing order – John Dews, Alan Wilkinson, Chris Pusey, Bob Kilby (ret)

Heat 3: Soren Sjosten leads John Dews

Aces win 46 -32.   Peter Collins 12 from 4 rides. Soren Sjosten 11 paid 12.
Roger Jones made his debut as Team Manager for the Rebels with Bob Radford picking the team. Ulf Lovaas was absent and Rebels used Rider Replacement. Bob Kilby retired in heat 1 and scored zero points from 4 rides, breaking the tapes in his last heat; no doubt his performance cost the Rebels the match as usually he was Mr Reliable around Sandy Lane.

BELLE VUE ACES 1 August 1974 away at Oxford

Heat 1: John Davis, Gordon Kennett, Chris Pusey and Alan Wilkinson

Heat 1: John Davis, Alan Wilkinson and Chris Pusey

Heat 3: Chris Morton and Richard Greer

No Peter Collins (away to Denmark for the British-Nordic-American Final) and the Rebels pip a win 40-38. Soren Sjosten 12 from 5 rides. Chris Pusey 8 paid 9. Chris Morton 6 paid 9. Reserves Ian Hindle (Exc-0-0) and Alan Grinshaw (1-fell-tapes) had a poor night. Credit to the Aces though, they were 12 points down after Heat 6, clawed back a few then lost a few so still 12 points adrift after Heat 10, but two 5-1s and a 4-2 made it a nail-biter, especially as the "on for a max" Bob Kilby broke the tapes in Heat 12 and was excluded.

BELLE VUE ACES 28 June 1975 at home to Oxford

A 42-36 home win does not tell the tale of a hard fought battle. With the score at 13-5 and looking like the meeting was going to be walkover, Heat 4 saw a 5-1 to the Rebels and in the fastest time recorded at the track for 2 years (1/5th of a second outside the track record) by Dag Lovaas, with Gordon Kennett holding off Peter Collins and Geoff Pusey. Aces showed dominance again, with 5-1s in Heats 5 and 7.

12 points down, the Rebels managed a comeback in Heat 8 with a 5-1 to Kennet and Dews, a 3-3 in Heat 9, and Dag Lovaas riding consecutive heats by coming out again in Heat 10 for another 5-1 with Gordon Kennett over Soren Sjosten and Russ Hodgson. With only a 4 point lead, the Aces needed to step up, which they did in Heat 11 with a 4-2 to Peter Collins and Geoff Pusey (split by John Dews).

The Rebels were still fighting though and managed a 5-1 with Gordon Kennett and Dag Lovaas over Soren Sjosten and Alan Wilkinson in Heat 12 leaving only a 2 point lead to the Aces. This meant they could still lose or draw, but Peter Collins and Chris Morton faced no threats from Eddie Davidsson (2 points the whole night) and Trevor Geer (nil points from 5 rides at the end; also suffered an engine failure while in second place).

Rebels missed the skills of Richard Greer, who failed to score in Heat 1 then took no further part in the meeting, having injured himself in a fall. They were also unfortunate that Gordon Kennett (who scored 13 paid 15) had an engine failure in Heat 6 while otherwise zinging this night with pairing with Dag Lovaas.

BELLE VUE ACES 9 August 1975 at home to Oxford

Heat 1: Soren Sjosten, Dag Lovaas, and Helgi Langli

Speedway Star Knockout Cup – Aces win 45-33 (87-69 on aggregate). Peter Collins absent, the top scorers were Alan Wilkinson (10 paid 11) and Chris Morton (11 paid 12) and Doug Wyer guesting (9 from three heat wins, finishing last in Heat 11 behind Helgi Langli, Dag Lovaas and Geoff Pusey). John Dews was top scorer for the visitors with 11 from five rides (one heat win and 4 second places).

BELLE VUE ACES 9 August 1975 at home to Oxford (cont)

Heat 2: John Dews, Russ Hodgson, Geoff Pusey and Trevor Geer

Heat 2: Russ Hodgson and John Dews

Heat 3: Chris Morton, Paul Tyrer, Paul Gachet, Richard Greer

BELLE VUE ACES 9 August 1975 at home to Oxford (cont)

Heat 4: John Dews, Russ Hodgson, Doug Wyer (G) and Gordon Kennett

Heat 4: Russ Hodgson and John Dews

Heat 5: Paul Tyrer, Dag Lovaas, Chris Morton, Helgi Langli

COVENTRY BEES

Brandon was one of the great stadiums – always a pleasure to visit. The Bees had a glorious history, 10 times Midland Cup winners between 1952 and 1979, 3 times Elite League Champions, and 6 times British League Champions.

Nigel Boocock

Ole Olsen 1976

Alan Molyneux 1976

Mitch Shirra 1976

BRITISH FINAL, BRANDON STADIUM, 30 July 1975

Doug Wyer, Martin Ashby, Dave Jessup and Gordon Kennett

Sadly, the stadium has gone but such happy memories here

CRADLEY UNITED

Boring name - "United" - always remembered as "Cradley Heathens". Dudley Wood Stadium (never easy to find in the days before SatNav) first provided speedway in 1947. A very faithful fanbase and their supporters at away matches were always vocal and created a great atmosphere.

Howard Cole

Steve Bastable

John Boulger

Bernt Persson

CRADLEY UNITED At home to Oxford 8th June 1974.

Looking like a certain defeat to the dominant Rebels, United never had a lead and were even 8 points down by Heat 5. In no small part to the returning Ulf Lovaas using his knowledge from a season earlier and scoring 10 paid 11. But the riders rallied with a 4-2 (John Boulger and Arthur Price) in Heat 12 and a 5-1 in Heat 13 (Howard Cole and Bruce Cribb) for the final score 39-39.

Heat 1: Ulf Lovaas (yb), Arthur Price, Bob Kilby (w), John Boulger

Heat 2: Mal Corradine, Trevor Geer (yb), Russ Osborne, John Dews (w)

CRADLEY UNITED At home to Oxford 8th June 1974.

Heat 2: Mal Corradine, Trevor Geer (yb)

Heat 2: Russ Osborne, Mal Corradine, John Dews (w)

Heat 3: Dave Younghusband, Bruce Cribb, Richard Greer (yb). Gordon Kennett (w)

CRADLEY UNITED At home to Oxford 8th June 1974.

Heat 3: Bruce Cribb, Richard Greer (yb).

Heat 8: Arthur Price, Ulf Lovaas (w), Russ Osborne, Trevor Geer (yb)

CRADLEY UNITED At home to Oxford 8th June 1974.

Heat 9: Russ Osbourne and John Davis

Heat 10: Gordon Kennett and John Boulger

CRADLEY UNITED At home to Oxford 26 April 1975.

As in the previous year, the United needed last heat intervention to prevent a home loss. A 5-1 by Bernie Persson and Bruce Cribb over (up to then unbeaten) Dag Lovaas and Rickard Hellsen turned a two point deficit (35-37) into a two point win (40-38). Only twice in the match had the home side had a lead so the Cradley fans really cheered their riders at the end.

Heat 1: Dag Lovaas (w), Arthur Price, Richard Greer (yb) and John Boulger

Heat 2: Russ Osborne, John Dews (yb), Dave Perks and Trevor Geer (w)

Heat 3: Dag Lovaas (w), Sandor Levai (exc Tapes), Rickard Hellsen (yb) and Bruce Cribb

EASTBOURNE EAGLES

Still racing at Arlington – no mean feat when so many stadiums have gone to developers. Sad news this year (2018) is the death of Bob Dugard, but the Dugard family continue his legacy. I never saw Bob race but I remember him as a promoter at Oxford with great affection. The Eagles produced many good riders in the 1970s.

Eric Dugard

Roger Abel

Colin Ackroyd

Steve Naylor

EASTBOURNE EAGLES

Mike Sampson

Colin Richardson

Pete Jarman

Dave Lanning

EASTBOURNE EAGLES

Steve Weatherley

Paul Gachet

Steve Weatherley

Eric Dugard

Keith Lawson

EASTBOURNE EAGLES   at home to Oxford 16 May 1976

Oxford may well have lost this match for being too twitchy at the gate – 4 exclusions for tape-breaking - and for, an otherwise on form, Mick Handley's engine failure.
Final score Eagles 41 Cheetahs 37.

Heat 1: Steve Weatherley and Carl Askew

Heat 2: Phil Bass, Steve Naylor, Colin Ackroyd, Roy Sizmore

Heat 3: Brian Leonard and Eric Dugard

EASTBOURNE EAGLES   at home to Oxford 16 May 1976

Heat 3: Brian Leonard and Eric Dugard

Heat 3: Brian Leonard (yb) Mal Corradine (w), Pete Jarman and Eric Dugard

Heat 3: Eric Dugard, Mal Corradine and Pete Jarman (and Brian Leonard's wheel)

EASTBOURNE EAGLES at home to Oxford 16 May 1976

Heat 4: Roy Sizmore, Colin Ackroyd, Phil Bass and Mike Sampson

Heat 5: Pete Jarman, Kevin Young (and Eric Dugard)

Heat 6 Colin Richardson and Phil Bass (yb)

EXETER FALCONS

Riding at the "wall of death" stadium with its steel barriers at the County Ground. A good home record of wins was always credited to visiting riders not wanting to chance a crash into the fence. Another in the long list of stadiums gone for development. The Falcons were good at using British talent (as any examination of notable Falcons will show) but their greatest asset was Ivan Mauger (1973 – 1977 and 1984).

Ivan Mauger

Scott Autrey

Scott Autrey and Tony Lomas

EXETER FALCONS

Geoff Mudge, Steve Reinke, Scott Autrey, and Kevin Holden

John Titman, Mike Farrell, Ivan Mauger

Away to Oxford 19 July 1975

EXETER FALCONS   Away to Oxford 10 July 1975

An overwhelming victory, where the Falcons took advantage of an understrength Rebels. A meeting where Dag Lovaas fell and retired hurt in a collision with teammate Trevor Geer (Heat 7), creating the opportunity for Scott Autrey and Kevin Holden to get a 5-1 and bring the teams level at 21-21. Neck and neck but the final three heats went 5-1, 4-2, 4-2 for a 43-35 Falcon victory.

Coin toss for gates. Glynn Shailes oversees Ivan and Gordon Kennett

Mike Farrell and Ivan Mauger

EXETER FALCONS   Away to Swindon 8 May 1976

Snatching victory from the Robins in a Heat 13 effort from Ivan Mauger and John Titman getting a 5-1 to end the meeting 39-39. Exeter had a non-scoring Les Rumsey (2 x tapes break) and Swindon's Bobby McNeil had two retirements with engine problems.

For both sides, a "what-if" match.

Heat 3: Phil Herne and Geoff Bouchard

Heat 5: Phil Herne, Geoff Bouchard, Ivan Mauger, and Bobby McNeil

HACKNEY HAWKS

One cannot divorce the name Len Silver from Hackney – once a rider and then a promoter. Rider parades to the theme from "The Magnificent Seven" and hearing that music will always raise a nostalgic tear among fans.

Barry Thomas 1976

Zenon Plech 1976

Keith White 1976

Dag Lovaas 1974

Dave Morton 1976

Trevor Hedge

HACKNEY HAWKS   at home to Oxford 2 Aug 1974

An immaculate Barry Thomas, unbeaten in his 4 rides and guest rider Chris Pusey scoring 9 from 3 rides then engine problem retirement in his last race, gave the Hawks their 41-37 victory. In only 4 heats did a Rebel take the chequered flag in first place (Kilby x 3; Dews x 1). The Hawks were never behind and kept the Rebels under their thumb.

Heat 3: Hugh Saunders, Richard Greer, Bob Kilby and Dave Morton

Heat 4: Chris Pusey and John Dews

HACKNEY HAWKS at home to Oxford 2 Aug 1974

Heat 4: John Dews, Chris Pusey and Dave Kennett

Heat 7: Bob Kilby (yb) and Dave Kennett

HACKNEY HAWKS   away to Oxford 6 June 1974

Dominant Hawks, lead by Phil Crump (Guest) and Dag Lovaas, whitewashed the Rebels 44-34. Dag unbeaten and Phil only beaten once (by Gordon Kennett in Heat 13). Fantastic evening for Laurie Etheridge, riding at 7, who scored 8 paid 11.

Heat 2: Laurie Etheridge and John Dews

Heat 2: Laurie Etheridge, John Dews and half of Dave Morton

Heat 3: Hugh Saunders and Richard Greer

HACKNEY HAWKS away to Oxford 6 June 1974

Heat 4: Laurie Etheridge and Dag Lovaas

Heat 6: Dave Morton, Dag Lovaas and Ulf Lovaas

Richard Greer and (I think) Geoff Maloney

HACKNEY HAWKS   away to Oxford 3 July 1975

A Rebel victory 44-34, with an off-night for the Hawks. Top scorers: Dave Kennett 7, and Dave Morton 7 paid 8. In only 3 heats did a Hawk take the chequered flag first – the two Daves and Barry Thomas.

Dave Kennett

Heat 3: Dave Kennett and Richard Greer

Dave Kennett

HACKNEY HAWKS   away to Oxford 3 July 1975

Christer Lofqvist

Heat 5: Barry Thomas leads John Dews and Eddie Davidson

Heat 5: Barry Thomas and Eddie Davidson

HACKNEY HAWKS away to Oxford 3 July 1975

Heat 5: John Dews and Mike Broadbank

Heat 6: Christer Lofqvist and Ted Hubbard

HALIFAX DUKES

The nickname was taken from the Duke of Wellington's regiment, stationed in Halifax. The elephant they wore on their bibs was also a link to the regiment (I guess a military link to India where Wellesley, before a Dukedom, made his name as a commander).

Although with a shortage of silverware in the trophy cabinet (best season was possibly 1966 when they were BL Champions, KO Cup Winners, and Northern Cup Winners), they enjoyed huge local support.

Eric Boocock

Charlie Monk

Away to Oxford 21 August 1975:
Heat 1: Helgi Langli, Rick France (yb), Charlie Monk (w) and Dag Lovaas

Heat 1: Dag Lovaas leads, Rick France (yb), Charlie Monk (w) and Helgi Langli

HULL VIKINGS

Speedway returned to Hull in 1971 after a long absence, racing at the Boulevard, which was better known as the home ground of Rugby League Club – Hull F.C. (since gone to developers). Most famous Vikings who raced here in the 1970s include Ivan Mauger (1978-81), Barry Briggs (1976) and Egon Muller (1976).

Jim McMillan

Bobby Beaton in action at Leicester

Heat 1: Barry Briggs and Paul Gachet
Away to White City 31 May 1976
Viking thrash the Rebels 44.5 to 33.5 in the absence of Dag Lovaas

HALIFAX DUKES away to White City 31 May 1976

Heat 2: Rickard Hellsen, Graham Drury (w) and Jack Millen

Heat 3: Bobby Beaton (w) and Richard Greer

IPSWICH WITCHES

A successful club over many years (mid 70s to mid 80s), they raced at Foxhall Stadium, which originally had been built for speedway. The track became shorter when stock racing was introduced and a new speedway track laid inside their track. John Louis is perhaps their most famous rider (although this might be challenged by fans of Tomasz Gollob, Mark Loram and Tony Rickardsson – all World Champions in their time but not while Witches) and he went on to promote the Witches.

John Louis

Billy Sanders

Mick Hines

IPSWICH WITCHES   Away to Oxford 11 July 1974

The Witches cast a spell over Oxford with a 48-30 victory. Nine times an Ipswich rider took the chequered flag in first place, creating four 5-1s and three 4-2s, plus five drawn heats. Earlier, the Witches had hammered the Rebels at Foxhall 50-28 in the Speedway Star KO Cup (19th April 1974). They would finish the season at No3, behind Exeter and Belle Vue.

John Louis

Billy Sanders

Heat 1: Bob Kilby and Olly Nygren

IPSWICH WITCHES Away to Oxford 11 July 1974

Heat 2: Trevor Jones (w), Mick Hines (yb), and Trevor Geer
(This looks like a pull up from a stopped race for false start)

Heat 2: Trevor Geer, Trevor Jones (w) (and Neil Middleditch)

IPSWICH WITCHES Away to Oxford 11 July 1974

Heat 2: Trevor Geer and Trevor Jones (w)

Heat 3: Billy Sanders (yb) and John Davis

IPSWICH WITCHES   Away to Oxford 11 July 1974

Heat 4: Tony Davey (W), Ulf Lovaas and Trevor Geer

Heat 5: John Louis (w), John Davis, Richard Greer and Olly Nygren

KING'S LYNN STARS

A pretty impressive list of riders over the years – Terry Betts, Malcolm Simmons, Michael Lee, Dave Jessup, then more recently than the period concerned in this book, Darcy Ward, Tony Rickardsson.

Malcolm Simmons

Terry Betts

Adi Funk

David Gagen

KING'S LYNN STARS

Paul Tyrer

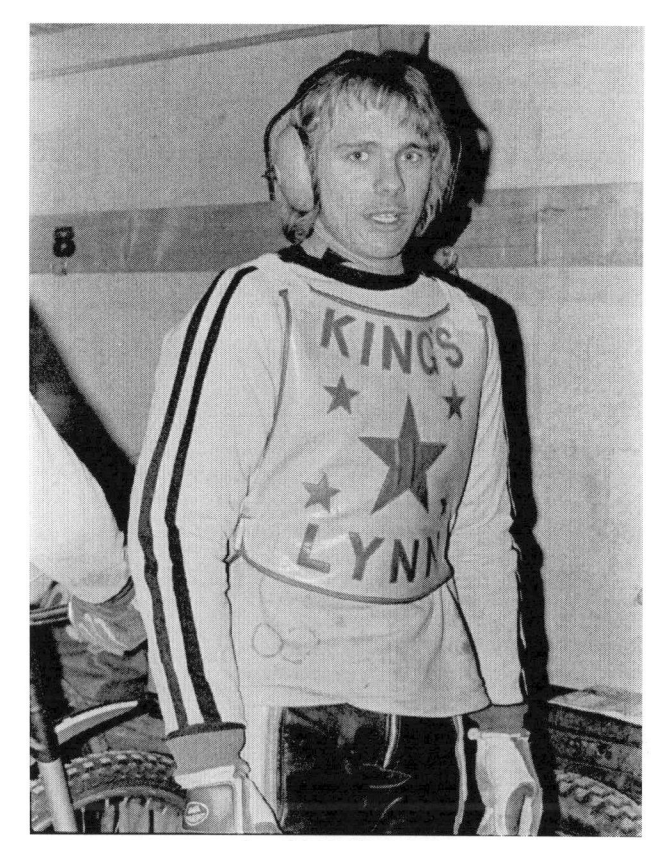

Jan Henningsen

Michael Lee

Terry Betts

KING'S LYNN STARS   At home to Oxford 25th May 1974

Four points down after Heat 3, the Stars pulled level with a 5-1 then went backwards with a 1-5. They trailed the visitors until Heat 10 when a 5-1 from Terry Betts and Ian Turner gave them a two point lead. Heats 11 and 12 kept that lead with Malcolm Simmons then Terry Betts pulling off first places for draws and a fantastic Heat 13 from Malcolm and Barry Crowson produced a 5-1 to nail the final score at 42-36.

Heat 1: John Dews (yb), Terry Betts, Ian Turner, and Bob Kilby

Heat 1: Terry Betts and Bob Kilby (look at the fence!)

Heat 2: Richard Greer and Ray Bales (and the programmes shield the fans' face from shale)

KING'S LYNN STARS At home to Oxford 25th May 1974

Heat 2: Richard Greer

Heat 2: Bobby McNeil

Heat 3: Eddie Reeves, Gordon Kennett, Bob Humphreys, Ulf Lovaas

Heat 3: Eddie Reeves, Gordon Kennett, Bob Humphreys, Ulf Lovaas

KING'S LYNN STARS At home to Oxford 25th May 1974

Heat 3: Gordon Kennett

Heat 3: Ulf Lovaas

Heat 3: Gordon Kennett

KING'S LYNN STARS   At home to Oxford 25th May 1974

Heat 4:

Heat 4: John Davis

Heat 5: Bob Kilby (w) and John Dews (yb)

Heat 5: John Dews and Eddie Reeves

KING'S LYNN STARS At home to Oxford 25th May 1974

Heat 6: John Davis, Ian Turner, Terry Betts

Heat 6: John Davis and Terry Betts

KING'S LYNN STARS At home to Oxford 25th May 1974

Heat 6: Terry Betts

Heat 8: Richard Greer (yb), John Dews (w) and Ian Turner

Heat 9: Richard Greer, Barry Crowson, John Davis and Eddie Reeves

LEICESTER LIONS

Yet another stadium gone, in its time Blackbird Road was a premier stadium (like Brandon) for bigger events than just league matches.

Ray Wilson

Dave Jessup

Frank Auffret

Ray Wilson and Dave Jessup

LEICESTER LIONS   At home to Oxford 4 June 1974

A satisfying home win 46-32 – both Dave Jessup and Ray Wilson unbeaten and Frank Auffret 9 paid 10. Oxford's highest scorer was Richard Greer with 7 paid 9.

Heat 1: Malcolm Ballard

Heat 2: Bobby McNeil

Heat 2: Norman Storer and Keith White

Heat 2: Norman Storer, John Dews (yb), Keith White and Bobby McNeil (w)

97

LEICESTER LIONS   At home to Oxford 4 June 1974

Heat 3: Richard Greer (yb), Frank Auffret, Mick Bell and Gordon Kennett (w)

Heat 3: Richard Greer (yb), Frank Auffret,

Heat 3: Gordon Kennett (w) and Richard Greer (yb)

LEICESTER LIONS   At home to Oxford 4 June 1974

Heat 4: John Dews (yb) and Norman Storer

Heat 4: Ray Wilson, John Dews (yb), John Davis (w) and Norman Storer

Heat 5: Bob Kilby (w), Ulf Lovaas (yb) and Frank Auffret

LEICESTER LIONS   At home to Oxford 4 June 1974

Heat 5: Ulf Lovaas (yb) and Malcolm Ballard

Heat 5: Bob Kilby

Heat 5: Dave Jessup

Heat 5: finish

LEICESTER LIONS At home to Oxford 4 June 1974

Heat 6: Dave Jessup, John Davis (w), Malcolm Ballard and Bobby McNeil (yb)

Heat 7: Ray Wilson, Richard Greer (yb), Gordon Kennett (w) and Keith White

Heat 8: John Dews (yb), Malcolm Ballard (behind) and Norman Storer

LEICESTER LIONS   At home to Oxford 4 June 1974

Heat 9: John Davis (w), Richard Greer (yb) and Frank Auffret

Heat 10: Dave Jessup

Heat 10 Richard Greer

Heat 10: Dave Jessup, Richard Greer (w), Malcolm Ballard (and Gordon Kennett)

LEICESTER LIONS   At home to Oxford 4 June 1974

Heat 10: Gordon Kennett

Heat 10: Gordon Kennett

Heat 11: Ray Wilson, Ulf Lovaas (yb), Keith White and Bob Kilby (w)

Heat 11: Bob Kilby (w) and Ulf Lovaas (yb)

LEICESTER - Blackbird Road - World Cup Semi-Final 21 May 1974

Ist John Louis   2nd Peter Collins   3rd Reg Wilson   4th Bob Valentine   5th Barry Briggs

Heat 1: Martin Ashby (yb), Peter Collins (w) and Barry Briggs

Heat 1: Peter Collins (w) and Barry Briggs

Heat 2: Reg Wilson (yb), Ivan Mauger, Phil Herne, (and Bob Kilby)

LEICESTER - Blackbird Road - World Cup Semi-Final 21 May 1974

Heat 3: Eric Broadbelt, John Louis, Doug Wyer and Chris Pusey

Heat 4: Billy Sanders, George Hunter and Bob Valentine

Heat 5: Bob Kilby (w), Eric Broadbelt (yb) and Barry Crowson

LEICESTER - Blackbird Road - World Cup Semi-Final 21 May 1974

Heat 6: Phil Herne (yb), Barry Briggs (w), George Hunter and Chris Pusey

Heat 8: John Louis (w), Billy Sanders (yb) Reg Wilson, and Martin Ashby

Heat 8: Martin Ashby

106

LEICESTER - Blackbird Road - World Cup Semi-Final 21 May 1974

Heat 10: John Louis and Bob Kilby

Heat 10: Barry Briggs (yb) and Bob Kilby

Heat 13: Arnie Haley (yb), John Louis, Ivan Mauger and George Hunter (w)

NEWCASTLE DIAMONDS

Which great riders haven't raced with a diamond on their bib? Newcastle was often the starting point for some great careers – Ivan Mauger, Ole Olsen, Anders Michanek, Dag Lovaas and current superstar Nicki Pedersen. A popular duo were the brothers, Joe and Tom Owen.

Joe Owen

Tom Owen

Rob Blackadder

Ron Henderson

NEWCASTLE DIAMONDS

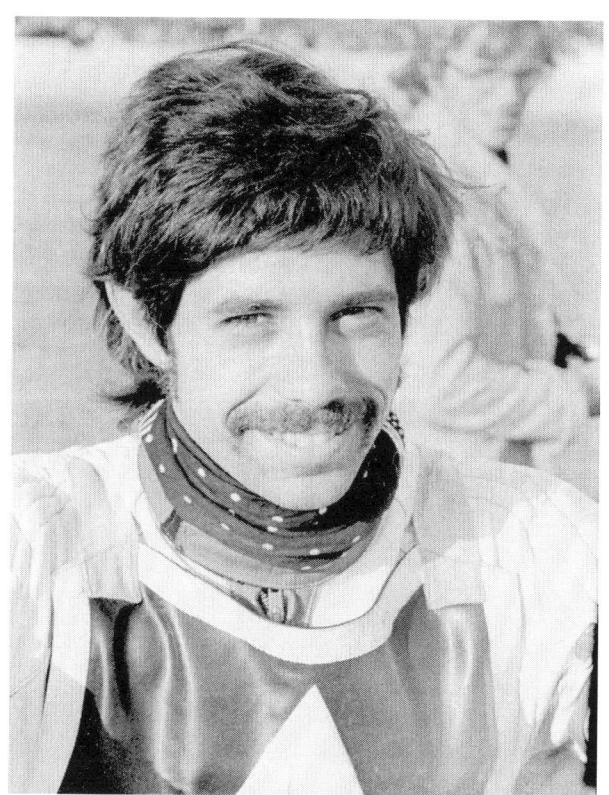

Phil Michaelidies

Brian Havelock

Tim Swales

Andy Cusworth

NEWCASTLE DIAMONDS away to Weymouth 22 July 1975

A bit of a bashing for the Wizards, going down 34 – 44 (the Owen brothers taking 23 points themselves).

Heat 1: Chris Robins, Tom Owen (w) and Bryan Woodward

Tom Owen

Heat 3: Joe Owen (w), Nigel Couzins, and Robbie Blackadder

110

NEWCASTLE DIAMONDS away to Weymouth 22 July 1975

Heat 5: Tom Owen (w), Nigel Couzins, Ron Henderson

Heat 7: Joe Owen and Melvyn Soffe

NEWCASTLE DIAMONDS away to Oxford 6 May 1976

Crunching 48-30 win over the Cheetahs. Coming from behind (6 points down after Heat 3) the Diamonds then only lost one heat (Heat 10, a 5-1 to Carl Askew and Mick Handley) taking five 5-1s and four 4-2s.

Heat 1: Ron Henderson (yb), Tom Owen (w), Carl Askew (and Jim Wells)

Heat 1: Tom Owen spills...    ...and brings down Carl Askew

Heat 1: Ron Henderson and Carl Askew

112

NEWCASTLE DIAMONDS away to Oxford 6 May 1976

Heat 3: Brian Havelock and Phil Bass

Heat 4: Joe Owen

Heat 4: Joe Owen and Brian Leonard

NEWPORT WASPS

In fact, the nickname "Wasps" had been dropped in 1972 but old habits die hard and every team needs a nickname – where's the glamour in just being known as "Newport"? Nice to see the name restored in recent years.

Phil Crump

I took so few photos of Newport as Oxford and they hardly met each season,
The riders who wore a Newport bib have appeared elsewhere in this book under other clubs so I decided not to duplicate. Apologies to Newport fans for the dearth.

Bob Kilby and Neil Street
away to Oxford 20 June 1974

Never behind at any stage, Newport had terrific performances from Reidar Eide (9 paid 10), Roy Trigg (8), and Phil Crump (unbeaten 12). Oxford, on the other hand, struggled to get their act together, with exclusions, falls and tape-breaking.

OXFORD CHEETAHS

My team :-)   I started following in the 1960s and, with the blip of Rebeldom, was covering their resurrection in 1976 in the New National League (Lawson, K. 2018 "The Cheetahs 1976 – The Resurrection" lulu.com).

Carl Askew

Mick Handley

Mal Corradine

Harry Maclean

OXFORD CHEETAHS

Steve Holden

Roy Sizmore

Brian Leonard

Colin Meredith

For more: "The Cheetahs 1976 – Resurrection"   lulu.com/shop

OXFORD CHEETAHS

Gerald Smitherman

Martin Yeates

David Shield

Pip Lamb

Jim Wells

Phil Bass

OXFORD REBELS

In 1973, the second year the team were known as Rebels, I started my minor journalistic career and worked alongside the management, mostly as Trackside Photographer 1974 and 1975 (Lawson, K. 2018 "Rebels 1975 – The Last Season" Lulu.com". It was a privilege to serve the sport we all love and, forty+ years on, to be able to bring back memories for people.

Bob Kilby

Hasse Holmqvist

Rick Timmo

John Dews

Colin Gooddy

Pete Jarman

OXFORD REBELS

Ulf Lovaas

Gordon Kennett

Dag Lovaas

Paul Gachet

John Davis

Rickard Hellsen

OXFORD REBELS

Trevor Geer

Henk Steman

Helgi Langli

Eddie Davidsson

Neil Middleditch

Colin Richardson

PETERBOROUGH PANTHERS

Promoted by Danny Dunton, the Panthers raced in the National League and provided riders, such as Richard Greer, to Oxford Rebels. In more recent times, it has fielded in the team, Mark Loram, Troy Batchelor, Jason Crump, Sam Ermolenko, and Gary Havelock so its golden years postdate the period of this book.

Brian Clark

Tony Featherstone

1976

POOLE PIRATES

Today, the Pirates have an enviable record of success but in the 1970s not a lot happened for them.

Malcolm Simmons

Malcolm Ballard

Neil Middleditch 1976

Eric Broadbelt 2018

John Davis and Pete Smith

POOLE PIRATES Away to Oxford 9th May 1974 (Spring Gold Cup)   Oxford 41 – Poole 37

A terrible first bend accident in Heat 3 ended Odd Fossengen's career. Trevor Geer was loaned to the Pirates in place of Colin Gooddy and scored 8 (paid 9) for them. Poole top scorers were guest riders, Phil Crump (14) and Nigel Boocock (7). Mike Cake replaced Bruce Cribb, scoring 5.

Heat 1: John Dews, Mike Cake (hidden), Phil Crump (w) and Bob Kilby

Heat 3: Odd Fossengen (w), Ulf Lovaas, Antony Woryna (yb) and Gordon Kennett

I visited Odd in the Radcliffe, taking him magazines etc and this photo, before he was ambulanced closer to home to recover. He was amazingly stoic about the accident.

POOLE PIRATES   Away to Oxford 8 August 1974

An absolute thrashing for the boys from the south coast – Rebels 52 Pirates 26.

Heat 1: John Davis and Colin Gooddy

Heat 1: John Davis and Colin Gooddy

Heat 1: John Davis and Pete Smith

POOLE PIRATES   Away to Oxford 8 August 1974

Heat 2: Paul Gachet and Dingle Brown (w)

Heat 3: Bob Kilby, Richard Greer, Richard May (w) , Antony Woryna (yb)

Heat 4: Trevor Geer, Eric Broadbelt (yb) , and Brian Clark (w)

POOLE PIRATES   Away to Oxford 8 August 1974

Heat 5: Colin Gooddy

Heat 6: John Dews and Pete Smith (yb)

Heat 7: Gordon Kennett and Antony Woryna (yb)

READING RACERS

I used to enjoy (as a fan) going to Tilehurst up to 1973 and having a couple of beers in the Bell after the match. The Racers resumed in 1975 at Smallmead, which previously had been a refuse tip. Not much in the trophy cabinet (BL Champions 1973) in the 70s, but good crowds.

Anders Michanek

Bengt Janssen

Dave Jessup

Mick Bell

Richard May

John Davis

READING RACERS Away to Oxford 17 July 1975 (Challenge Match)

With the absence of Anders Michanek (Mick Bell moved up from 7 and replaced there by Barney Kennett) the Racers went down 34 – 44. Bengt Janssen scored 12 from 5 rides.

Heat 2: Paul Gachet and Richard May

Heat 2: Barney Kennett

Heat 3: Gordon Kennett and John Davis

READING RACERS Away to Oxford 17 July 1975 (Challenge Match)

Riders emerge from pits for Heat 3
Eddie Davidsson (left) John Davis (w), Gordon Kennett, and Bob Humphreys (yb) on bike

Coming out for Heat 4: Richard May and Dag Lovaas

READING RACERS Away to Oxford 17 July 1975   (Challenge Match)

Heat 4: Richard May (yb) and Dag Lovaas

Heat 4: Trevor Geer and Bengt Janssen (finishing 1st and 2nd respectively

READING RACERS   Home to Oxford 4 August 1975 (Gulf British League)

A narrow margin win 41 – 37 over the Rebels (missing Hasse Holmqvist and using Rider Replacement). Barney Kennett came in at Rebel 7 but failed to score. John Dews fell in his first 2 races and although he managed a heat win in his third, he wouldn't score again. The Racers had leadership performance from Anders Michanek (maximum) and Bengt Janssen (11) with every member of the side on the scoreboard.

Anders Michanek

Heat 1: Anders Michanek

Heat 2: Bernie Leigh, Trevor Geer, Barney Kennett and Richard May

131

READING RACERS Home to Oxford 4 August 1975

Heat 3: John Davis and Richard Greer

Heat 3: Richard Greer (yb), John Davis, Bob Humphreys and Dag Lovaas

Heat 3: Dag Lovaas, John Davis, Richard Greer

READING RACERS Home to Oxford 4 August 1975

Heat 4: Richard May, Trevor Geer, Bengt Janssen and Barney Kennett

Heat 4: Gordon Kennett and Bengt Janssen

READING RACERS Home to Oxford 4 August 1975

Heat 5: Richard Greer (w) , John Davis, John Dews (yb)

Heat 5: John Dews (yb) going down as John Davis dives under him

READING RACERS Home to Oxford 4 August 1975

Heat 6: Anders Michanek, Trevor Geer (yb), Mick Bell, and Gordon Kennett (w)

Heat 6: Anders Michanek and Gordon Kennett (w)

READING RACERS   Home to Oxford 4 August 1975

Heat 7: Dag Lovaas (w) , Bengt Jansson, Richard May (and Gordon Kennett)

Heat 8: John Dews (yb) and Bernie Leigh

SHEFFIELD TIGERS

Faithful to Owlerton Stadium, which has avoided closure and redevelopment, since it was built in 1929. Reg Wilson would make 470 appearances for the Tigers. Another team with not much silverware (BL KO Cup 1974).

Doug Wyer

Reg Wilson

Chris Morton

Russ Hodgson

SHEFFIELD TIGERS   away to Oxford 26 June 1975

Against an on-form Oxford on their home track, the Tigers struggled, winning only 2 heats (2x 5-1) and drawing 5.

Doug Wyer scored 11 and Chris Morton 10 (both having 5 rides). Reserves Taffy Owen and Nicky Allott scoring only 1 point between them.

Captains Gordon Kennett and Doug Wyer do a coin toss for gates, supervised by Glynn Shailes

Heat 1: (L-R) John Dews, Russ Hodgson (w), Richard Greer

Heat 1: Russ Hodgson (w) and Richard Greer

SHEFFIELD TIGERS away to Oxford 26 June 1975

Heat 1: Craig Pendlebury (yb) and John Dews

Heat 2: Trevor Geer, Nicky Allott (yb) and Taffy Owen (w)

Heat 4: Trevor Geer, Dag Lovaas, Doug Wyer and Nicky Allott

SWINDON ROBINS

Currently there is some talk about a new stadium but, otherwise, have been at Blunsdon since 1949. Three riders always pop up in my mind when I think of the Robins – Martin Ashby, Barry Briggs and Bob Kilby (Kilby, L. 2017 "To the Heart of Kilb) .

Martin Ashby

David Ashby

Bobby McNeil

Bob Kilby

Martin Ashby

140

SWINDON ROBINS

David Ashby and Geoff Bouchard

Martin Ashby and Mike Broadbank

SWINDON ROBINS   At home to Oxford 13 July 1974 (25th Anniversary Challenge)

Before the match for real, there was fun on a sponsor's mopeds.

Robins had a zero scoring Mick Handley at No2, David Ashby at No7 scoring 1 from 4 rides. Up against Rebels with guest Mick Bell at No6 being their top scorer with 9 points.

Final Score Robins 36, Rebels 42

Martin Ashby

Not a clear photo but can see the fans

Martin Ashby, Gordon Kennett and Richard Greer

SWINDON ROBINS At home to Oxford 13 July 1974 (25th Anniversary Challenge)

Heat 1: Bob Kilby (w), Martin Ashby, Gordon Kennett (yb) and Mick Handley

Heat 3: Ed Stangeland, Richard Greer (w) , Mike Keen and John Davis (yb)

Heat 3: Richard Greer (w) and Mike Keen

SWINDON ROBINS At home to Oxford 13 July 1974 (25th Anniversary Challenge)

Heat 3: Ed Stangeland, John Davis (yb) and Richard Greer (w)

Heat 3: Ed Stangeland and John Davis (yb)

SWINDON ROBINS At home to Oxford 13 July 1974 (25th Anniversary Challenge)

Heat 4: Norman Hunter, Geoff Bouchard (yb) and Ulf Lovaas

Heat 4: Ulf Lovaas (w) and Norman Hunter

SWINDON ROBINS At home to Oxford 13 July 1974 (25th Anniversary Challenge)

Heat 5: Bob Kilby (w) and Ed Stangeland

Heat 5: Gordon Kennett (yb) and Mike Keen

SWINDON ROBINS Midland Riders QR 14 May 1975

Result: 1st Bob Kilby.   2nd Bob Valentine.   3rd Martin Ashby   4th Dag Lovaas

Heat 1: Dag Lovaas (yb), Bob Valentine (w) and Norman Hunter

Heat 1: Bob Valentine (w) and John Dews

Heat 2: Geoff Bouchard, Bobby MacNeil (and Martin Ashby's leg)

SWINDON ROBINS   Silver Plume 6 August 1975

These photos have been scanned from colour negatives in very poor condition.

Heat 1: Ray Wilson (w) and Phil Herne

Heat 2: Nigel Boocock, Barry Thomas, Martin Ashby and Bobby McNeil

Heat 3: Phil Crump, Reidar Eide, and Dag Lovaas

Heat 4: Peter Collins

Result: 1st Peter Collins   2nd Martin Ashby   3rd Ray Wilson   4th Phil Crump

SWINDON ROBINS Silver Plume 6 August 1975

Heat 5: Dag Lovaas and Geoff Bouchard

Heat 5: Dag Lovaas, Martin Ashby and Norman Hunter

SWINDON ROBINS At home to Exeter 8 May 1976   39-39

Heat 3: Phil Herne (w) and Geoff Bouchard

Heat 5: Phil Herne (yb) , Geoff Bouchard, Ivan Mauger (w) , and Bobby McNeil

Looks like Heat 2: David Ashby, Geoff Mudge , and Soren Karlsson

After Heat 12, the Robins had the score at 38 – 34, then the Falcons managed a 5-1 for the draw with Ivan Mauger (15 from 5 rides) and John Titman (7 and 2 bonus points).

WEYMOUTH WIZARDS / WILDCATS

Bryan Woodward

Chris Robins

Vic Harding

Nigel Couzins

151

WEYMOUTH WIZARDS / WILDCATS

Martin Yeates

Melvyn Soffe

Danny Kennedy

WEYMOUTH WIZARDS / WILDCATS

Geoff Swindells

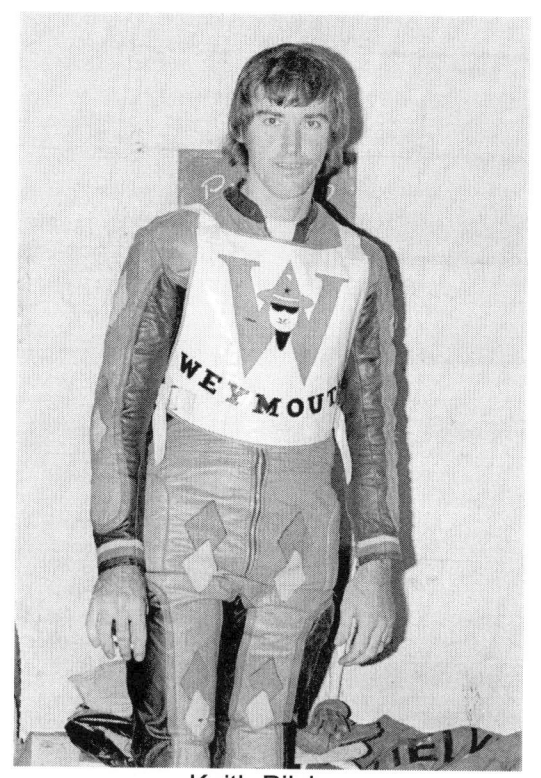

Keith Pilcher

Ricky Owen

Roger Stratton

WEYMOUTH WIZARDS at home to Newcastle 22 July 1975 (see also Newcastle pages)

Wizards lose 34 - 44

Heat 4: Melvyn Soffe, Vic Harding and Brian Havelock

Heat 4: Melvyn Soffe and Vic Harding

Heat 4: Melvyn Soffe

WEYMOUTH WIZARDS at home to Newcastle 22 July 1975

Heat 4: Phil Michaelidies (yb), Vic Harding, Melvyn Soffe and Brian Havelock (w)

Heat 4: Vic Harding

Heat 6: Tim Swales (yb) and Chris Robins

WHITE CITY REBELS 1976

Under a threat of stadium closure, promoters Danny Dunton and Bob Dugard moved the Rebels down the A40 to White City in 1976. It was a stadium that hosted big events but it never quite worked for league speedway in this era.

The White City carpark and pits entrance on Press Day 1976

Blue Peter filmed on Press Day (Peter Purves)

The White City Rebels 1976 (Team Manager Lee Dunton)

WHITE CITY REBELS 1976   Press Day

Peter Purves (of Blue Peter)

Trevor Geer

Rickard Hellsen

Gordon Kennett

Gordon Kennett

WHITE CITY REBELS 1976

Dag Lovaas

Gordon Kennett

John Dews

Paul Gachet

Richard Greer

Rickard Hellsen

WHITE CITY REBELS

Trevor Geer

Tommy Jansson, Linda Haydn (actress) and Gordon Kennett on the opening night (John Dews in frame as well)

White City v Wimbledon 24 March 1976 Heat 1
Tommy Jansson, Trevor Geer, Barry Crowson, Dag Lovaas

White City v Wimbledon 24 March 1976 Heat 2
Rickard Hellsen, Larry Ross, Paul Gachet, Roger Johns

WIMBLEDON DONS

Plough Lane was one of the top stadiums and, sadly, is lost to us. The Dons are probably one of the most successful British teams of all time. Run out a list of names – Barry Briggs, Ivan Mauger, Bert Harkins, Gary Middleton, Ronnie Moore, Malcolm Simmons.

Barry Briggs

Ed Stangeland

Reg Luckhurst

Trevor Hedge

WIMBLEDON DONS

Bo Jansson (1976)

Larry Ross (1976)

Mick Hines (1976)

Roger Johns (1976)

WIMBLEDON DONS Away to Oxford 12 April 1974

Heat 8: Bert Harkins, John Dews and Rick Timmo

Bert Harkins

Barry Briggs

Heat 8: Bert Harkins, John Dews and Barry Briggs

WIMBLEDON DONS   Away to Oxford 12 April 1974

Heat 8: Barry Briggs and John Dews

Heat 8: Bert Harkins and Barry Briggs on the way to their second 5-1

Reg Luckhurst (yb) Neil Cameron (?) and Gordon Kennett

Despite good scores from Barry Briggs (11) and Bert Harkins (10) the rest of the team did not contribute much (4 falls, 2 engine failures, and 2 tape-breaking). Final score 34-43 (Rebels).

WIMBLEDON DONS Away to Oxford 25 August 1975 (a double match day)

Heat 1: Helgi Langli, Dag Lovaas, Barry Briggs and the wheel of Larry Ross

Heat 1: Helgi Langli, Dag Lovaas, Barry Briggs

Heat 2: Barry Crowson, Trevor Geer, Reg Luckhurst, and John Dews

NB More detail in "Rebels 1975 – The Last Season"

WIMBLEDON DONS   Away to Oxford 25 August 1975 (a double match day)

Heat 2: Reg Luckhurst and Trevor Geer

Heat 3: Edgar Stangeland and Richard Greer

Heat 4: John Boulger (G), Barry Crowson, John Dews and Gordon Kennett

John Boulger guested for the missing Tommy Jansson and was the Dons highest scorer with 12 from 5 rides. Barry Briggs scored 9 paid 10. Rebels won 44-34.

WIMBLEDON DONS   At home to Oxford 25 August 1975   42-35

This was the second meet of the day on a Bank Holiday – first leg at Oxford.

Coin toss for gates: Barry Briggs and Gordon Kennett

Heat 1: Dag Lovaas the only rider to beat Barry Briggs this match

Six heats were drawn. Oxford suffered with the new boy Helgi Langli on zero points – a more experienced rider in the team might have brought the Rebels an away win. Two 5-1s to the visitors compared to only one for the Dons. It was their three 4-2s plus a 5-0 in heat 13 (Lovaas fell and Greer had been excluded on the 2 minute rule, having had to recover from a ride in heat 12. Tommy Jansson the only unbeaten rider of the night.

PLOUGH LANE, WIMBLEDON Wills Internationale 27 May 1974 and 26 May 1975

Sorting a box of negatives and it's difficult to know which year is which as rider set-up and heats almost identical. So apologies for the lack of certainty.

Anders Michanek

John Louis

Dag Lovaas

Ole Olsen

PLOUGH LANE, WIMBLEDON Wills Internationale 27 May 1974 and 26 May 1975

Dag Lovaas (1975)

Anders Michanek

Ivan Mauger and Tommy Jansson (likely this is 1975)

I think that is Ivan Mauger falling (1974)

Ivan Mauger (1974)?

PLOUGH LANE, WIMBLEDON Wills Internationale 27 May 1974 and 26 May 1975

Ivan Mauger 1975

Tommy Jansson

Ray Wilson (1975)

Reidar Eide and Barry Briggs (1974)

(1975) Martin Ashby, Phil Crump, Jim McMillan, Dag Lovaas

PLOUGH LANE, WIMBLEDON Wills Internationale 27 May 1974

1974 Winner – Peter Collins

WOLVERHAMPTON WOLVES

Monmore Green was founded in 1928 and the team has on and off seasons for various reasons over the decades.

Finn Thomsen

George Hunter

Ole Olsen

Ole Olsen

171

WOLVERHAMPTON WOLVES

My drawing in the programme for Oxford v Wolves 4 July 1974.

Bob Radford and Glynn Shailes sit down to a meal of roast wolf. It was a tease as the Wolverhampton programmes would have cartoons in the same vein. On this occasion, Ole Olsen failed to turn up and the Wolves lost 31-47.

WOLVERHAMPTON WOLVES

George Hunter and Gary Peterson 1975

Gary Peterson 1975

George Hunter 1974

POOLE PIRATES 2016

Poole Pirates at start of 2016 season

Chris Holder

Chris Holder

Davey Watt

Brady, Davey and Hans

Brady Kurtz

Brady Kurtz

174

POOLE PIRATES 2016

Kryzysztof Buczkowski

Kryzysztof Buczkowski

Hans Anderson

Hans Anderson

Kyle Newman

Kyle Newman

SWINDON ROBINS 2018

The 2018 squad at the beginning of the season

Nick Morris

Nick Morris

SWINDON ROBINS 2018

Zach Wajtknecht

Zach Wajtknecht

David Bellego

David Bellego

177

SWINDON ROBINS 2018

Mitch Davey

Mitch Davey

Troy Batchelor

Troy Batchelor

SWINDON ROBINS 2018

Tobiasz Musielak

Tobiasz Musielak

Adam Ellis

Adam Ellis

Visit the **National Speedway Museum** at Paradise Wildlife Park, Broxbourne, Herts.

Best time to go is the WSRA Annual Event in early Spring (check the WSRA page on Facebook for details). Meet riders from past and present.

Rebels 1975 - The Last Season
By Keith Lawson
View this Author's Spotlight
Paperback, 180 Pages ☆☆☆☆☆ This item has not been rated yet

Prints in 3-5 business days

A unique collection of over 300 photos recalling the final year of Oxford Rebels (1975) - the riders, the races, the champions. With references and photos of all the British League teams that year. Plus the results of the matches with individual riders' scores.

The Cheetahs 1976 - The Resurrection
By Keith Lawson
View this Author's Spotlight
Paperback, 208 Pages ☆☆☆☆☆ This item has not been rated yet

Prints in 3-5 business days

A unique collection recalling the year in which the Cheetahs were resurrected after the stadium nearly closed. Numerous photos illustrate the facts of the matches as well as some stories of the fight to save and preserve Cowley Stadium.

Available from lulu.com/shop [NB check the website for special offers, e.g. free postage].

What people think of these books:

"Just received 'Rebels 1975 - The Last Season' (as well as 'The Cheetahs 1976 - The Resurrection') as a gift. Tremendous and a very well researched book and well worth adding to my already extensive collection of speedway books. Plenty of statistics and photos from the author with many personal anecdotes and contemporary quotes. Well worth purchasing both books for anyone interested in the shale sport and Oxford Speedway in particular as they very much complement each other during a transitional period at Cowley." Steve Roberts

"Your books are great, full of wonderful material to provoke memories, have been reading them all week." Marcos Young (journalist).

"Thanks for your book, I'll be reliving 1975 all over again!" Barry Cross (Hotcrossdesign.co.uk)

"Two very good books - really enjoy seeing the pics and reading the insights into both seasons especially the 1976 rescue season. The match details brought back so many good memories. A must for every speedway supporter." John Fray

"Just got "Rebels1975-The Last Season" and ordered "The Cheetahs 1976" today. Remember the contents as if they were yesterday!! You can almost smell the Castrol-R and hear the roar of the bikes in those old pictures." John White

This book has been sponsored by Nytex   www.nytexmemoryfoam.co.uk enabling the publishers to keep the retail at the lowest possible price.
When you need a good mattress, please check this business out

Danny Dunton – rider and promoter – who welcomed me into the Rebels family as Trackside Photographer at Oxford. I had to decline his invitation to cover Peterborough and White City as it was too expensive for me to travel weekly to those tracks but I so wish I had been able.

Printed in Great Britain
by Amazon